Discovering
South
America

BOLIVIA

Discovering South America

BOLIVIA

LeeAnne Gelletly

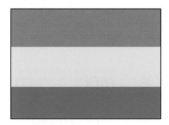

Mason Crest Publishers
Philadelphia

Produced by OTTN Publishing, Stockton, N.J.

Mason Crest Publishers
370 Reed Road
Broomall, PA 19008
www.masoncrest.com

3 5 7 9 8 6 4 2

Library of Congress Cataloging-in-Publication Data

Gelletly, LeeAnne.
  Bolivia / LeeAnne Gelletly.
      p. cm. — (Discovering South America)
  Includes bibliographical references and index.
  ISBN 1-59084-291-X
  1. Bolivia—Juvenile literature. I. Title. II. Series.
  F3308.5 .G45 2003
984—dc21

                                            2002011894

Discovering
South
America

Argentina		Paraguay
Bolivia	**South America:**	Peru
Brazil	Facts & Figures	Suriname
Chile	Ecuador	Uruguay
Colombia	Guyana	Venezuela

Table of Contents

Discovering South America

James D. Henderson

South America is a cornucopia of natural resources, a treasure house of ecological variety. It is also a continent of striking human diversity and geographic extremes. Yet in spite of that, most South Americans share a set of cultural similarities. Most of the continent's inhabitants are properly termed "Latin" Americans. This means that they speak a Romance language (one closely related to Latin), particularly Spanish or Portuguese. It means, too, that most practice Roman Catholicism and share the Mediterranean cultural patterns brought by the Spanish and Portuguese who settled the continent over five centuries ago.

Still, it is never hard to spot departures from these cultural norms. Bolivia, Peru, and Ecuador, for example, have significant Indian populations who speak their own languages and follow their own customs. In Paraguay the main Indian language, Guaraní, is accepted as official along with Spanish. Nor are all South Americans Catholics. Today Protestantism is making steady gains, while in Brazil many citizens practice African religions right along with Catholicism and Protestantism.

South America is a lightly populated continent, having just 6 percent of the world's people. It is also the world's most tropical continent, for a larger percentage of its land falls between the tropics of Cancer and Capricorn than is the case with any other continent. The world's driest desert is there, the Atacama in northern Chile, where no one has ever seen a drop of rain fall. And the world's wettest place is there too, the Chocó region of Colombia, along that country's border with Panama. There it rains almost every day. South America also has some of the world's highest mountains, the Andes,

Dusk settles over La Paz and Mount Illimani, Bolivia's second-highest peak.

and its greatest river, the Amazon.

So welcome to South America! Through this colorfully illustrated series of books you will travel through 12 countries, from giant Brazil to small Suriname. On your way you will learn about the geography, the history, the economy, and the people of each one. Geared to the needs of teachers and students, each volume contains book and web sources for further study, a chronology, project and report ideas, and even recipes of tasty and easy-to-prepare dishes popular in the countries studied. Each volume describes the country's national holidays and the cities and towns where they are held. And each book is indexed.

You are embarking on a voyage of discovery that will take you to lands not so far away, but as interesting and exotic as any in the world.

(Opposite) A woman peers inside a thatched hut on the Altiplano, or high plains. This immense plateau extends across southwestern Bolivia and southern Peru at a height of about 11,975 feet (3,650 meters). (Right) Sunset over Titicaca, the second-largest lake in South America, as seen from the Island of the Sun.

1 A Land at the Top of the World

¡HOLA! ARE YOU discovering Bolivia? It's the highest of the South American republics and—with the largest percentage of Native Americans— a land of ancient and colorful traditions. In Bolivia, snowy mountain peaks and dry, elevated plateaus contrast with tropical lowland plains and humid Amazon jungles. Boats ply the waters of lazy, meandering rivers and the world's highest navigable lake, but never dock at a Bolivian ocean port.

A Landlocked Country

Pacific waves once lapped against the shores of Bolivia, but now the country is one of two landlocked nations in South America (the other is Paraguay). The fifth-largest nation on the continent, triangular-shaped Bolivia extends over an area of approximately 425,000 square miles (1.1 million square kilometers), about the size of Texas and California combined. Its greatest north-south distance is 900 miles (1,448 km); its greatest east-west distance, 800 miles (1,287 km). Completely surrounded by its neighbors, Bolivia borders Argentina to the south, Chile and Peru to the west, Brazil to the north and east, and Paraguay to the southeast.

Bolivia's geography can be divided into four major areas: the Andean Highlands, the Valles (high valleys), the Yungas (lower valleys), and the tropical lowlands, referred to by the Spanish word for east, *Oriente*.

The Andean Highlands

Although two-thirds of Bolivia's land lies to the east of the Andes, South America's great mountain system, the majority of Bolivians live in the mountainous western third of the country, at elevations of up to 15,000 feet (4,500 meters). Three of Bolivia's largest five cities are situated on the *Altiplano* (high plain), an immense plateau that runs through the country from the north Peruvian border southward to the Argentine boundary.

Two parallel mountain ranges, or *cordilleras*, of the Andes border the Altiplano: the Cordillera Occidental to the west and the Cordillera Oriental to the east. The Cordillera Oriental contains some of the highest peaks of the central Andes, including Mount Illimani (21,201 feet, or 6,462 meters). Illimani towers over the Altiplano city of La Paz, Bolivia's administrative capital. The country's tallest peak, Nevado Sajama, reaches 21,463 feet (6,542 meters) above sea level near the Chilean border.

Visitors to Bolivia's highlands often find themselves breathless, and not just from views of majestic mountains. Because of reduced amounts of oxygen in the thin air of the plateau—which averages 12,000 feet (3,658 meters) above sea level—new arrivals have trouble breathing and can suffer altitude sickness.

The high plateau itself is a dry, even arid place with few trees. At its northern edge Bolivia's largest lake (and South America's second largest) borders Peru. Jointly controlled by the two nations, Lake Titicaca is—at 12,500 feet (3,813 meters)—the world's highest navigable lake. Titicaca measures an enormous 145 miles (233 km) long and 60 miles (97 km) wide.

A large house is perched in the rocky Cordillera Oriental mountain range, which contains some of the highest mountains in Bolivia.

The major river of the Altiplano, the Desaguadero, flows south from Lake Titicaca to the shallow Lake Poopó. Much of the land in this southern region of the Altiplano consists of salt plains and dry wilderness. South of Poopó lies Salar de Uyuni, the world's largest salt flat. Once part of a prehistoric salt lake covering most of southwestern Bolivia, Salar de Uyuni now produces almost 20,000 tons of fine salt per year.

The Valles

South and east of the Cordillera Oriental, the land slopes down into the Valles, or upper valleys, area, which is known for fertile soil and a temperate climate. Wildlife, subtropical forests, and lush vegetation thrive on the steep slopes of the Valles—sometimes referred to as the central highlands—while cities such as Cochabamba, Sucre, and Potosí flourish in its broad basins. Farms that dot the fertile land of this south-central part of Bolivia produce most of the country's food.

The Yungas

To the northeast of the Cordillera Oriental lies the Yungas, or lower valleys, region. Somewhat isolated because of its many deep gorges and dense semitropical forests, this sparsely populated region was first settled by the Spanish because of its large gold deposits. Today its rich slopes produce coffee, sugarcane, citrus fruit, bananas, and coca (a tropical shrub whose leaves are chewed to alleviate altitude sickness, but which are also refined to make the illegal drug cocaine).

The Oriente

From the heights of the mountains and valleys, the land drops down close to sea level, forming tropical lowlands in northern and eastern Bolivia. In the northern part of the Oriente lie the meandering rivers and tropical rain forests of the Amazon Basin, while the slightly drier region to the south contains woods and flat prairie, as well as swamps.

Many tributaries of Brazil's Madeira River, including the Beni, Guaporé, and Mamoré, flow through the thick tropical jungles and swampy marshland of the Oriente. Because of its marshy terrain, much of the area suffers from heavy flooding during the rainy season.

Covering more than three-fifths of Bolivia, the hot, flat Oriente is much less densely populated than the Altiplano. However, the discovery of natural

Quick Facts: The Geography of Bolivia

Location: Central South America, bordering Argentina to the south, Brazil to the north and east, Chile to the west, Paraguay to the southeast, and Peru to the west

Area: (about the size of California and Texas combined)
  total: 424,162 square miles (1,098,580 sq. km)
  land: 418,683 square miles (1,084,390 sq. km)
  water: 5,479 square miles (14,190 sq. km)

Borders: Argentina, 517 miles (832 km); Brazil, 2,113 miles (3,400 km); Chile, 535 miles (861 km); Paraguay, 466 miles (750 km); Peru, 559 miles (900 km)

Climate: varies according to altitude: hot and humid in low tropical regions, cold and dry at high elevations.
  dry season: May through October
  rainy season: November through March

Terrain: Andes Mountains, highland plateau (Altiplano), upper and lower valleys, and lowland plains of Amazon Basin

Elevation extremes:
  lowest point: Río Paraguay—295 feet (90 meters)
  highest point: Nevado Sajama— 21,463 feet (6,542 meters)

Natural hazards: flooding during March and April in the northeast

Source: Adapted from CIA World Factbook, 2001.

gas and oil deposits in the region, as well as strong timber and agricultural growth, has brought rapid development, particularly in the former frontier town of Santa Cruz.

Climate

The weather in Bolivia varies according to the region and elevation—from humid and tropical in the northern lowlands, to temperate in highland valleys, to harsh, semiarid, and cold on the Altiplano. Snow remains on the highest peaks of the Andes year-round.

For the most part, the tropical lowlands of the Oriente stay hot and wet year-round, with an average temperature of 75°F (24°C). During the winter, however, cold winds blowing from the south, called *surazos*, can cause a significant drop in temperature.

In the upper and lower valleys of the Andes, the annual average temperature ranges from 60°F to 70°F (16°C to 21°C). Rain falls frequently in the steamy Yungas, regardless of the normal rainy season, while residents of the less humid Valles enjoy mild temperatures and an ideal climate, especially in the winter.

An Aymara man holds a small llama in this photo, taken in the Lake Titicaca area. Historians believe the llama was domesticated some 4,000 years ago.

Because of its high elevation, the Altiplano is mostly cool, with an average year-round temperature of 50°F (10°C). During the summer months of December, January, and February (because Bolivia is in the Southern Hemisphere, its seasons are opposite those in the United States), weather on the plateau may be hot during the day but cool at night. Because the air is so dry, little snow falls during the winter, although temperatures often reach freezing.

Most of the rain falls during the summer months in Bolivia, with the rainy season lasting from November through March. On the Altiplano much of the runoff flows into Lake Titicaca, so the surrounding land remains dry; droughts are common on the high plateau, especially during the winter months of May to September.

Bolivia's Rich Variety of Wildlife

Wildlife that is common to Bolivia includes the jaguar, maned wolf, tapir, spider and howler monkeys, ocelot, giant anteater, tapir, caiman (South American crocodile), and condor. Most of these can be found in one of Bolivia's largest nature reserves, the Noel Kempff Mercado National Park. Located in the Amazon Basin, its savanna, forests, and rain forests are home to approximately 4,000 species of plants, more than 600 bird species, and many endangered species.

Two domesticated animals native to the Andes have provided meat, transportation, and clothing to Bolivian civilizations for centuries: the llama, which is similar to a camel, and the somewhat smaller alpaca, which is like a sheep but with long, silky wool. The *vicuña*, a wild relative of these domesticated species, roams Bolivia's Altiplano.

(Opposite) Sculptured heads protrude from a stone wall at Tiwanaku, the site of a pre-Incan settlement near modern La Paz. (Right) President George W. Bush shakes hands with Bolivia's president, Jorge Quiroga. During Quiroga's December 2001 visit to the White House, the two leaders talked about global affairs and the relationship between their two countries.

2 A Turbulent History

SINCE ACHIEVING INDEPENDENCE, Bolivia has had at least 16 constitutions and nearly 200 revolutions and coups, many resulting in dictatorships. Even before the arrival of the Spanish in the 16th century, the area was long the site of periodic warfare, oppression, and empire building.

Pre-Columbian Civilization

One of the first Native American tribes to settle in Bolivia, the Chavíns, dominated the region from about 1400 B.C. to 400 B.C. Several hundred years later, a more advanced Indian civilization, the Tiwanaku (also spelled Tiahuanaco) arose. This tribe eventually established a prosperous empire that extended to present-day southern Peru, northern Chile, and much of the Bolivian highlands. Between A.D. 500 and 900, the Tiwanaku Indians, based

17

in their capital on the Altiplano near Lake Titicaca, colonized and traded throughout the south-central Andes.

The great city of Tiwanaku reflected the highly civilized society of its inhabitants. Skilled artisans created massive stone monuments and buildings of huge cut stone blocks, often decorated with gilded ornamentation and elaborate carvings. The Tiwanaku people raised crops such as corn and potatoes on rich lakeside lands, herded domesticated llamas and alpacas (which provided transportation, meat, and wool), and fished from reed boats on Lake Titicaca.

Around the year 900, the powerful empire of the Tiwanaku began to crumble, perhaps destroyed by the Aymara-speaking tribes invading from the north. The Aymara established many small villages in the highlands, where they prospered for several hundred years. Then, in the 1400s, Inca warriors from southern Peru marched into the area, intent on further expanding their huge, highly advanced empire. After overpowering the Aymara, the Incas forced their civilization on the defeated tribes, making them speak the Incan language—Quechua—and follow the Incan religion, as well as pay tribute to the dominant empire.

But European discovery of the New World ensured that Inca control would not last long. Spanish *conquistadors* (conquerors), led by Francisco Pizarro and Diego de Almagro, sought land and wealth for themselves and for Spain. Within two years of reaching the Inca lands in 1531, the Europeans had vanquished the Incas and taken control of their empire. With the conquistadors came the Spanish language, the Roman Catholic religion, and Hispanic customs.

Spanish Colonial Rule

Spain referred to its new colony as Upper Peru, and in 1538 established La Plata as its capital. Just six years later, the discovery of an enormous deposit of silver ore in the mountains provided the Spanish conquerors with the wealth they sought. Thousands of European settlers poured into the area, where they founded the mining town of Potosí, took control of the lands, and enslaved thousands of Indians.

While the silver mines of Potosí yielded great fortunes for the Spanish, the Indians forced to work in them suffered. Many died from the brutal conditions in the mines or from lung disease. Determined to extract as much silver from the earth as possible, the Europeans turned to Africa for more slaves.

A modern-day Bolivian woman in traditional Inca costume.

Spanish rulers did little to develop the colony of *Alto Perú*, focusing mostly on creating and improving roads to more easily move their newly acquired mineral wealth. Meanwhile, an aristocratic upper class of landowning Spanish settlers evolved. At the same time, most *indigenous*, or native, people and those of mixed race worked as tenant farmers or toiled in the mines or smelting mills.

Independence and War

On May 25, 1809, the people of Chuquisaca (later renamed Sucre) revolted against foreign rule, sparking

Bolivia's namesake, Simón Bolívar (1783–1830), is one of the most famous figures in South America's history. Under the general's leadership, most of South America was freed from Spanish control. Bolivia declared itself independent in August 1825.

an independence movement. Their revolt was part of a generalized uprising against Spanish domination. By 1810 all of Spanish America—from Mexico in the north, to Argentina and Chile in the south—was in revolt against Spain.

In northern South America, General Simón Bolívar liberated Venezuela and Colombia. Bolívar then turned to Major General Antonio José de Sucre, who liberated Ecuador in 1822, and Peru (including Alto Perú) in 1824.

On August 6, 1825, the new nation proclaimed its independence and assumed the name Bolivia, in honor of Bolívar. After the passage of a new constitution in 1826, Sucre became Bolivia's first president.

The country's next president, General Andrés Santa Cruz, took office in 1829. Ten years later, in what would become an all-too-familiar occurrence in Bolivian politics, Santa Cruz was overthrown in a military coup. Political turmoil ensued. A seemingly endless series of military coups, revolutions, and dictatorships would overwhelm the nation for more than a century.

Meanwhile, neighboring countries jockeyed for pieces of Bolivia, eventually reducing by half the area held at the time of its independence. After a stinging loss to Chile in the War of the Pacific (1879–84), Bolivia gave up the Atacama Desert and its rich copper and nitrate deposits. That meant that Chile claimed Bolivia's 527-mile (850-km) coastline—its only outlet to the sea. In 1903 Brazil annexed Bolivia's northern Amazonian region, which was rich in rubber trees, while a war with Paraguay from 1932 to 1935 ended with Bolivia's loss of the Chaco Boreal, a lowland plain to the south thought to contain oil reserves.

During the 1900s Bolivia remained economically dependent on its mineral resources, especially tin (which replaced silver as a major export in the late 1800s). The mining industry was a big business, and rich mine owners dominated Bolivian politics. But they did little to improve the poor working conditions. In response, tin miners formed unions and attempted to strike for better conditions. Finally labor unrest led to the creation of a major political party supported by the miners—the Movimiento Nacionalista Revolucionario (MNR), or National Revolutionary Movement.

Revolution and Reform

In 1952 the MNR seized control of Bolivia from its military leaders, installing Víctor Paz Estenssoro as president of a civilian-run government. The MNR quickly instituted important reforms, extending

Hugo Banzer Suárez (1926–2002) was one of Bolivia's most influential leaders in the second half of the 20th century. He seized power in a 1971 coup and remained dictator until 1978. His regime used harsh measures to repress dissidents and opponents. Suárez returned to power in 1997, when he was elected president under the Bolivian constitution. However, health problems forced him to resign before he could complete his five-year term.

the right to vote to indigenous people and working to better the education and health of all Bolivians.

The new government seized the tin mines from private owners, creating the Mining Corporation of Bolivia (Corporación Minera de Bolivia—Comibol) and Bolivian Labor Federation (Central Obrera Boliviana—COB). The MNR also instituted agrarian reform that allowed tenant farmers, who were mostly Indians, to own their own property.

A military coup in 1964 ended the MNR's rule, and again a series of military governments took charge. In 1967, under one regime, the Bolivian army captured and killed Communist leader Che Guevara, who was trying to incite the common people of Bolivia to rebel against the government.

Return to Democracy

Under Bolivia's current constitution, passed in 1967 and revised in 1994, the country's president serves a five-year term in office. Members of Bolivia's Congress also serve five-year terms—senators, in the upper chamber of Congress; and deputies, in the lower. The highest court in the land is the Supreme Court, whose members are appointed by Congress.

But despite the 1967 constitution, an elected government did not really exist in Bolivia until 1982, when civil rule was finally restored and Hernán Siles Zuazo became president. The country was in economic chaos, suffering inflation that approached an annual rate of 3,000 percent. Miners called for nationwide strikes, and the price of tin, the country's major export, dropped dramatically.

Meanwhile, the United States was pressuring the government to eliminate illegal coca production. Since ancient times native people in the lands of modern-day Bolivia have regarded chewing the coca leaf, or drinking its tea, as a way of life. While coca use is legal in Bolivia, refining it into cocaine is not. Still, poor farmers in the Yungas and Upper Chapare regions (in the Amazon Basin) considered it a highly profitable crop when grown for illegal export.

During the 1980s Bolivia's democratically elected leaders took charge, instituting reforms to reduce high inflation and end corruption within many government-run businesses, including the mining industry. With the support of the United States, Bolivia introduced anti-drug-trafficking programs and began coca crop eradication efforts (aerial spraying of *herbicides* on coca plants). These efforts met with some success. By 2002, about 65 percent of the illegal coca cultivation worldwide had shifted to Colombia. Bolivia and Peru accounted for most of the remaining 35 percent.

While problems with inflation, severe poverty, social and labor unrest, and illegal drug production remain, reforms undertaken since the 1980s have led to some progress. And the government continues to prove its continued stability. In 2001, when Bolivian president Hugo Banzer Suárez resigned for health reasons, the vice president, Jorge Quiroga, assumed leadership of the country in a smooth, constitutional transition of power.

(Opposite) Workers prepare food to be shipped to grocery stores in Bolivia. Properly packaging food helps to ensure that food products are as safe and sanitary as possible. (Right) A young Bolivian girl sells vegetables from a makeshift stand.

3 Creating a Free-Market Economy

DESPITE ITS MINERAL wealth and many natural resources, Bolivia remains one of the poorest countries in Latin America. Economic development has not been easy, given the country's history of unstable governments, wars, and revolutions. An underfunded educational system, high inflation and unemployment rates, and labor unrest have also taken their toll. About 70 percent of Bolivians live below the poverty line.

During the 1980s and 1990s Bolivia's leaders worked to turn the failing government-regulated economy into a free-market one, in which prices are controlled by supply and demand, not governmental regulation. Many state-controlled businesses (such as the airline, communications, railroad, electric power, mining, and oil industries) were *privatized*—that is, sold to private investors. Bolivia signed a free-trade agreement with Mexico and joined Mercosur (Mercado Común del Sur, or Common Market of the South, which includes Argentina, Paraguay, Uruguay, and Brazil). Economic reform has proven successful, but Bolivia still has far to go in creating an economy that will reduce its severe poverty.

Dependence on Mineral Resources

Since the Spanish first laid claim to Bolivia, the land has produced immense mineral wealth. When the silver mines gave out in the late 1800s, tin took silver's place and Bolivia became one of the world's leading producers. In the 1980s, world market prices for tin dropped, but Andean mines still yielded other valuable minerals, such as antimony, copper, gold, lead, silver, tungsten, and zinc. These minerals became major Bolivian *exports*—products produced in the country that are sold to other nations.

Further development of the Oriente has led to the discovery of rich deposits of petroleum, natural gas, and iron manganese. In addition to helping fill Bolivia's energy needs, the oil and natural gas have become major exports.

Only about 3 percent of Bolivians work in mines, but mining accounts for approximately 13 percent of Bolivia's gross domestic product, or GDP (the total value of all goods and services a country produces annually). Another 7 percent of Bolivians work in manufacturing (including metal and petroleum refineries, food processing plants, and textile and jewelry factories), mainly at major industrial centers located in La Paz, Santa Cruz, and Cochabamba. Altogether, mining, mining-related industries, and manufacturing account for 31 percent of the country's GDP, but that number promises to grow in the 21st century.

Agricultural Riches

About half of Bolivia's people farm for a living, although farming provides just 16 percent of the nation's GDP. The rural farmers on the Altiplano eat much of what they raise—potatoes, beans, wheat, and *quinoa* (a hardy, high-protein grain that can survive the area's frequent frosts). Crops from the Yungas and the Valles, including soybeans, cacao, corn, and bananas, also usually end up in local markets. Some coffee from the Yungas is sold overseas, but most of Bolivia's agricultural exports come from large plantations in the eastern lowlands of the Oriente. Main agricultural exports from the Oriente region include soybeans, cotton, rice, sugarcane, beef, lumber, and rubber.

Bolivians work at a tin mine in Potosí. Tin and other mineral resources are an important component of Bolivia's economy.

A major, if illegal, Bolivian export is cocaine, produced by refining coca leaves. Certain experts estimate that as much as one-third of the Bolivian workforce is involved in some aspect of the illegal drug industry, with sales exceeding those of all other legal agricultural exports combined. Coca grown in the Yungas is used within Bolivia, while the Beni and Chapare regions of the Amazon Basin yield a substantial portion of the world's illegal coca crop.

The Bolivian government has engaged in coca eradication (spraying herbicides to destroy crops) and worked to stop drug shipments. Efforts have also been made to reduce coca production by offering incentives to poor farmers to grow substitute crops such as coffee, bananas, or *yuca* (cassava) instead of coca.

A peasant from the high plateau of the Andes feeds his cow. Agriculture employs about half of the people of Bolivia.

Quick Facts: The Economy of Bolivia

Gross domestic product (GDP*):
$8 billion (2001 est.)
GDP per capita: $1,025 (2001 est.)
Inflation: 4.4% (2000 est.)
Natural resources: tin, natural gas, petroleum, zinc, tungsten, antimony, silver, iron, lead, gold, timber, hydropower
Agriculture (16% of GDP): soybeans, coffee, coca, cotton, corn, sugarcane, rice, potatoes, timber
Industry (31% of GDP): mining, smelting, petroleum, food and beverages, tobacco, handicrafts, clothing, natural gas

Services (53% of GDP): stores, banks, transportation and communication companies; schools, hospitals, and government agencies; tourism
Foreign trade (1999 est.):
Exports—$1.26 billion: soybeans, natural gas, zinc, gold, wood.
Imports—$1.86 billion: capital goods, raw materials and semi-manufactures, chemicals, petroleum, food.
Currency exchange rate:
7.33 bolivianos = U.S. $1 (2002)

* GDP or gross domestic product—the total value of goods and services produced in a year.

Sources: CIA World Factbook, 2001; International Monetary Fund.

A Growing Service Economy

About 40 percent of Bolivia's workers provide services in a variety of jobs and professions, including retail businesses, banking, insurance, health, education, and government agencies.

Services that support the tourist industry are also providing an economic boost to the country. The rich archaeological heritage and fascinating landscape of Bolivia is attracting growing numbers of tourists, who bring money into the country to pay for food, lodging, transportation, guides, and souvenirs. More than half of Bolivia's GDP comes from the service industry.

Importance of Trade

Bolivia trades with the United States, Japan, and western European countries, as well as with fellow members of Mercosur. Some of the *imports* Bolivia buys from these countries include clothing, food, and household items; chemicals; and heavy machinery and transportation equipment.

For many years Bolivia benefited from a duty-free trade agreement with the United States. Established in 1991, the Andean Trade Preferences Act allowed Bolivia—as well as Peru, Colombia, and Ecuador—to sell certain goods to the United States without having to pay the usual tariff costs. The agreement attempted to provide more profitable legal alternatives to cocaine and heroin production and especially helped Bolivia's agricultural and timber producers and jewelry manufacturers.

Need for Improved Transportation

Bolivia's limited transportation system has hindered economic development. The country's rough terrain and thick forests have made it expensive and difficult to build roads and railway networks. Although paved highways connect the major population centers of La Paz, Santa Cruz, and Cochabamba, about 95 percent of all roads in Bolivia are unpaved. Travel by dirt road during the rainy season can be extremely difficult as many roads wash out.

Two major rail networks exist in the country: one in the east connects Santa Cruz with western Brazil and northern Argentina, and the other in the west connects La Paz, Cochabamba, and Oruro with northern Argentina and Chile. In northern Bolivia, major rivers such as the Mamoré, Beni, and Madre de Dios carry riverboats and barges, and serve as the area's transportation system. Air travel provides another method of transportation. More than 1,000 airports in Bolivia accommodate small aircraft, and international airports are located at La Paz, Cochabamba, and Santa Cruz.

A Challenging Future

Although 2.5 million Bolivians are in the labor force, the country's economy has not created enough jobs. By the end of the 20th century, unemployment hovered around 11.5 percent. Still, with its many resources of minerals, timber, and fertile land, Bolivia has great potential. Foreign investment and international loans should enable the country to further develop its industries, strengthen its transportation links, and improve the way of life of its people.

Since the early 1990s the United States has given money to support the eradication of coca farming in Bolivia as part of its so-called war on drugs. In December 2000, thousands of Bolivian farmers blocked roads to protest the eradication efforts, asking the government to help them grow alternative crops. The farmers pictured here were among 6,000 who spread coca leaves across a road near Chimore, in the Chaparé region.

(Opposite) A crowd of demonstrators gathers in La Paz at a political rally. The varied population of Bolivia is often enthusiastically involved in social and political issues. (Right) Shoppers visit a bazaar in front of the Cathedral of Nuestra Señora de la Paz (Our Lady of La Paz), which was built in the 1860s.

4 People of Ancient Traditions

MORE THAN 8 million people live in Bolivia, making it the eighth most populous nation in South America. About 8 in 10 Bolivians can claim at least some Native American ancestry: more than 50 percent of the country's people are American Indians, and another 30 percent are *mestizos* (of mixed white and Indian ancestry). Whites (of European descent) make up another 15 percent, while about 1 percent of the population is black, descended from African slaves forced to work the Potosí mines.

With its diverse population, Bolivia has three official languages—Spanish, Aymara, and Quechua. About half the populace speaks Spanish as a second language.

Quick Facts: The People of Bolivia

Population: 8,300,463

Ethnic groups: Quechua, 30%; Aymara, 25%; mestizo, 30%; white, 15% (figures rounded to whole numbers)

Age structure:
0—14 years: 38.5%
15—64 years: 57%
65 years and over: 4.5%

Population growth rate: 1.76%

Birth rate: 27.27 births/1,000 population

Death rate: 8.2 deaths/1,000 population

Infant mortality rate: 58.98 deaths/1,000 live births

Source: CIA World Factbook, 2001.

Life expectancy at birth:
total population: 64.06 years
male: 61.53
female 66.72

Total fertility rate: 3.51 children born per woman

Religions: Roman Catholic, 95%; Protestant (Evangelical Methodist, Quaker, and others)

Languages: Spanish, Quechua, Aymara (all official)

Literacy rate (age 15 and older): 83.1% (1995 est.)

*All figures are 2001 estimates, unless otherwise noted.

Rural Versus Urban Bolivia

Most of the people living in rural areas of Bolivia are Native American, mainly Aymara and Quechua Indians. Also referred to as *campesinos*, Bolivia's rural Indians scrape by as subsistence farmers, consuming most of what they produce. Over the centuries, few campesinos married outside their own community, so villages have maintained their distinct language, customs, and traditions.

The Aymara Indians make up about 25 percent of Bolivia's population. They live mainly in the northern part of the Altiplano or the Yungas, where they raise crops and herd llamas, alpacas, or sheep, using the wool to weave clothing or blankets, ropes, and household items. The Quechua, who comprise about 30 percent of Bolivia's people, live east of the Altiplano, in the valleys of southern Bolivia and in the cities of Cochabamba and Sucre. Many smaller Indian tribes also live in Bolivia, including the Guaranís and forest Indians of the more remote lowlands.

Most mestizos and whites populate the cities of the highlands or upper valleys. Toward the end of the 20th century, however, more Bolivians began migrating from farms to urban areas in search of jobs. Once-rural Bolivia is fast becoming increasingly urbanized; more than 60 percent of the population now lives in cities.

Religion and Education

The majority of Bolivians practice the Roman Catholic faith, which is Bolivia's official religion. Yet Protestant sects are growing, and in rural areas, where most Native Americans live, many Christian rituals commonly

Two Quechua boys wear wool hats, La Paz.

intermingle with *pre-Columbian* symbols and practices.

Education is free for children ages 6 to 14, but many children attend school for only a year or less. This is especially true in remote villages, where schools have little money. Still, the literacy rate has steadily improved over the years, reaching approximately 82 percent. Bolivia has several universities, including the Universidad de San Simón in Cochabamba and the Universidad Mayor de San Andrés in La Paz.

Food, Drink, and Clothing

Typical Bolivian meals consist mostly of meat dishes (beef, pork, poultry, or lamb), accompanied by rice, potatoes, and shredded lettuce. Main food

Members of the Bolivian national soccer team toss balls during a practice session before the 2001 Americas Cup competition. Soccer, or *fútbol*, is the favorite sport of most Bolivians.

sources in the highlands are the protein-rich quinoa grain, used as flour to make bread or thicken stews, and the potato, which may be dehydrated as *habas* and *cebada*.

Well-known local dishes include *empanadas salteñas* (a type of meat pie) and the *plato paceño* (a La Paz corn, bean, and potato specialty). Many Bolivian dishes feature various tuberous vegetables and flavorings such as **llajhua**, a hot sauce made from tomatoes and pepper pods. A hearty meal may be washed down with *api*, a thick drink of mashed corn, hot water, sugar, and cinnamon.

While whites and mestizos living in Bolivia's cities usually wear Western-style clothes, the typical garb of many indigenous people remains distinctly traditional. For women, it includes a dark-colored derby, or bowler hat (worn on the side if the woman is single, and on top if married), and a full *pollera* skirt, usually combined with a blouse, woolen sweater, and short jacket or shawl. Indian women also use an *ahuayo*, a colorful rectangular cloth that is slung across the back and tied around the shoulders, to carry produce, packages, and even small children.

Sports and Leisure

Like most other Latin Americans, Bolivians love soccer (*fútbol* in Spanish). Children and adults compete on local soccer fields, attend league matches in city stadiums, and passionately root for the national team during international competitions such as the World Cup or Copa América (America's Cup). The local highland teams competing at Estadio Hernando Siles in La Paz have the advantage of being used to playing in the thin air of its high elevation.

Bolivia is home to other lofty sports facilities as well, including the world's highest golf course, the Malasilla Golf Club, and the highest ski resort in the world, the Chacaltaya ski lift. Both can also be found near the city of La Paz.

National Holidays and Festivals

The Bolivian people celebrate eight national holidays, some religious and some political. Among the latter are Independence Day, celebrated on August 6 (the day independence from Spain was declared in 1825). Weeklong festivities often usher in major Roman Catholic holidays. These include Carnaval (Carnival), held a few days before Lent begins, and *Semana Santa*, or Holy Week, the week before Easter. Regional events often blend local folklore with national and Christian traditions.

Arts and Culture

Bolivia's pre-Columbian past can be seen in archaeological wonders such as the ruins of Tiwanaku, Samaipata, Incallajta, and Iskanwaya. Tiwanaku, the country's most important archaeological site, lies about 43 miles (69 km) west of La Paz. People marvel at the highland city's large stone structures, built from massive blocks that were precisely fitted together without mortar and then carved with distinctive designs and patterns. Several archaeological museums contain remnants of Bolivia's pre-Columbian heritage, in the form of gold and silver artifacts, pottery, and weaving.

Inca and Spanish traditions have blended in many areas of Bolivian arts, including sculpture, painting, literature, and architecture. The distinctive style, referred to as "Mestizo Baroque," can be seen in the paintings of Melcho Pérez Holguín and in colonial palaces and churches, such as the Iglesia de San Francisco in La Paz.

Practical use and art combine in the handwoven textiles created by rural Bolivian women, who learn the craft of spinning and weaving at a young age. With wool from llama, alpaca, and sheep, they create beautiful fabrics using colors, patterns, and figures representative of the region. Weavings may be made into ponchos, skirts, *ahuayos*, or colorful costumes.

Bolivia's regional folk music is distinctive and varied, much of it having evolved from pre-Inca, Inca, Spanish, Amazonian, and African influences. Traditional Andean musical instruments include the stringed *charango* (similar to a ukulele) and *violín chapaco*; the woodwind *quena* (reed flute) and **zampoña** (pan flute); and drums. Folk music is performed at fiestas and *peñas*, folk music clubs.

An Aymara man wears a colorful costume in a carnival parade. The people of Bolivia often go all-out to celebrate national and religious holidays.

Bolivians live in a variety of homes, from bustling cities to quiet rural areas. (Right) This farm dwelling is located on the Río Guapay, near Santa Cruz. (Opposite) Slums in the Barrio el Alto overlook La Paz, Bolivia's second-largest city.

5 Rapid Growth in Urban Centers

BOLIVIA IS DIVIDED into nine departments (similar to states or provinces): Beni, Chuquisaca, Cochabamba, La Paz, Oruro, Pando, Potosí, Santa Cruz, and Tarija. Many are named for major cities of the country.

La Paz

Bolivia has two capitals. La Paz serves as the administrative capital, housing government buildings and the presidential palace.

A major political and commercial center, La Paz is Bolivia's second-largest city, with a population of more than 800,000. The world's highest capital, the city is located on the Altiplano more than 2 miles (3.2 km) above sea level. It sprawls along the floor and up the sides of a narrow basin, creating a bowl-shaped metropolis of modern high-rise buildings and small traditional dwellings.

La Paz, seen here with Mount Illimani in the background, is the world's highest capital city.

Alonso de Mendoza founded the city on October 20, 1548, under the name of La Ciudad de Nuestra Señora de La Paz (The City of Our Lady of Peace). By the late 1800s it had become an important economic and transportation center. Today major businesses found in La Paz include importing and exporting companies, food canneries and beer distilleries, textile factories, and cement manufacturers.

El Alto

Just north of La Paz on the Altiplano lies the city of El Alto, formerly a suburb and shantytown of La Paz. In just 20 years, the rural area surrounding La Paz's international airport grew into Bolivia's fourth-largest city, with a population of more than 700,000. El Alto attracts many

A couple strolls through a narrow street in La Paz. The crowding of the city can be seen in the background.

campesinos who leave the countryside in search of jobs. Some find local employment as street vendors, auto mechanics, or seamstresses, while others ride buses to jobs in the factories, stores, and homes of La Paz.

Oruro

Located in the southern part of the Altiplano, north of Lake Poopó, the mining town of Oruro has more than 200,000 residents, making it Bolivia's fifth-largest city. The discovery of silver in nearby hills led to its founding in 1606; when the silver boom faltered in the 1800s, rich deposits of copper and tin boosted the town's economy.

Known as the folkloric capital of Bolivia, Oruro has an extremely large indigenous population: about 90 percent of its residents claim pure Indian heritage. Almost all the men work in the mines, earning a hard and hazardous living. A welcome break comes at Carnaval time, when Oruro hosts the largest annual celebration in Bolivia, featuring parades, folk music, and folk dancing.

Sucre

Named after the revolutionary hero Antonio José de Sucre, Bolivia's sixth-largest city has a population of more than 150,000 residents. Bolivia's constitutional capital, Sucre houses the nation's Supreme Court. The government provides jobs for many city residents. Others work on nearby farms or in food-processing factories, oil refineries, or cement-manufacturing facilities.

Sucre has undergone a series of name changes. Founded as La Plata in 1538, the city served as the capital of the Spanish colony of Upper Peru, evolving into a religious and cultural center. Later it was renamed Chuquisaca, which is known as the site where the uprising against Spanish rule began in May 1809. In 1825, the city was renamed to honor the independence fighter and first president of Bolivia. Sucre, a popular tourist attraction, contains many well-preserved examples of colonial architecture. Among them are the city's cathedral, completed in 1553, and the University of San Francisco Xavier, founded in 1624.

Cochabamba

Bolivia's third-largest city, Cochabamba (pop. 800,000) sits in a mountain valley beneath the towering peak of *Cerro* Tunari. With its warm, sunny days and cool nights, the prosperous city has an ideal, temperate climate. Area farmers raise corn, barley, wheat, and alfalfa, as well as fruits, in the fields around the market town. Industries in the city process fruits and vegetables, refine oil, and manufacture textiles.

The town was founded along the banks of the Rocha River in January

Cerro Palado, a mountain peak, looms over this street in Potosí. The city was founded in 1545.

1574 by Sebastián Barbe de Padilla. Its name comes from the Quechua words *khocha* and *pampa* (meaning "swampy plain"). Grains and cattle raised in the surrounding fertile valley provided food for Potosí miners during the silver boom, which earned Cochabamba its nickname: the breadbasket of Bolivia.

Potosí

The discovery of a major silver deposit in Cerro Rico ("Rich Hill") led to the founding of Potosí in 1545. Located at an altitude of about 13,780 feet (4,200 meters), the mining town is one of the highest cities in the world. With a population of more than 135,000, it is Bolivia's eighth-largest city. By the end of the 18th century, during the silver boom, the city contained about 200,000 residents, making it the largest city in the Western Hemisphere at the time. Today, miners extract tin, lead, and copper from Potosí mines, while others work in the factories that manufacture furniture, process beverages, and make electrical equipment.

Santa Cruz

Around the turn of the 21st century, the rapidly growing city of Santa Cruz became the largest city in Bolivia. This commercial and industrial hub of the eastern lowlands increased in population from 697,300 in 1992 to more than a million in 2002. More growth is likely, since the region provides most of Bolivia's agricultural exports, and chief industrial ones, such as natural gas and petroleum, are still being developed.

Founded in 1561 in the center of the country, east of the Cordillera Oriental foothills, Santa Cruz served mainly as an agricultural and cattle center. In the 1950s it began to grow as an industrial hub as well when highways linked the city with other major centers, and a railway to Brazil opened up.

A Calendar of Bolivian Festivals

Most Bolivian festivals celebrate religious holidays (honoring a Christian or Indian saint or god) and historical events, such as a famous battle. Festivities often include a combination of rituals, games, folk music, dancing, processions, feasts, and fun.

January

January 6 is **Día de los Reyes** (Kings' Day, or Epiphany). This Catholic holiday commemorates the visit of the Three Kings to the baby Jesus.

Ekeko, the Inca household god of abundance, is celebrated on January 24 during **Alasitas** (The Festival of Abundance). During the fair, street vendors sell miniatures of items that people would like to get in the coming year. The buyers place the tiny replicas on plaster images of Ekeko, in hopes that the god will make their wishes come true.

February

From February 2 to 5, the people of Copacabana celebrate the **Fiesta de la Virgen de Candelaria**. The weeklong festival, which centers on a black wooden image of the Virgin Mary, the patron saint of the city, includes both solemn rituals and hearty merrymaking.

Bolivians across the nation mark the beginning of Lent (the 40 days between Ash Wednesday and Easter) with **Carnaval** celebrations that include lively processions of music and merrymaking. One of the best-known celebrations is **La Diablada**, or Dance of the Devils, held in Oruro beginning the Saturday before Ash Wednesday. In parades and dance performances, elaborately costumed

participants portray angels and devils, historical characters, and Andean deities.

March

Early in the month, villagers in Tarabuco host one of Bolivia's largest festivals, **Phujllay** (pronounced pookh-yai), which in the Quechua language means amusement or play. More than 60 surrounding communities participate in local costume, celebrating the Battle of Lumbati, fought on March 12, 1816. The two-day fiesta includes Quechua Mass and processions, folk music, and dances.

April

Semana Santa, or Holy Week, may fall in March or April. Celebrations take place throughout the country as part of Easter Week, including Holy Thursday, Good Friday, and Easter Sunday.

May

La Fiesta de la Cruz (The Festival of the Cross), held May 3, is a religious celebration of music and parades remembering the cross upon which Christ was crucified. Tarija, Vallegrande, Cochabamba, and Copacabana host the best-known festivities.

Día de la Madre (Mother's Day) celebrations are observed on May 27. Cochabamba's celebration, **Heroínas de la Coronilla**, honors the women and children who defended the city during an 1812 battle in the war for independence.

One of La Paz's major festivals, **La Festividad de Nuestro Señor Jesús de Gran Poder**, held in late May or early June, rejoices in "the great power of

Jesus Christ." The fiesta features elaborately embroidered costumes and performances of Aymara folk and Inca ceremonial dances.

June

June 24 marks the feast day of **San Juan Bautista** (St. John the Baptist), considered the patron saint of the Amazon.

July

The last day of the month marks the first day of the **Fiesta del Santo Patrono de Moxos**, a colorful celebration honoring the sacred protector of the rural Indian village of San Ignacio de Moxos.

August

On August 6, many nationwide celebrations commemorate the country's declaration of independence from Spain, but the **Independence Day** fiesta at Copacabana is the biggest, celebrated the whole first week of August. It includes parades, brass bands, and fireworks.

With folk music and dance, the city of Quillacollo in the Cochabamba department celebrates **La Asunción de la Virgen de Urcupiña** on August 15. The fiesta commemorates a local shepherd girl's vision of the Virgin Mary and Child at Calvario Hill, as well as the subsequent appearance of a stone image of the Virgin, known as the Virgen de Urcupiña (also spelled Urkupiña).

September

The dogs have their day in a canine parade through the streets of Tarija during the **Fiesta de San Roque**, which celebrates the patron saint of dogs, whose official feast day is September 16. The fiesta is an eight-day festival featuring traditional music performances and a glittering parade of dancers.

October

The **Fiesta de las Flores**, or Flower Festival, in Tarija is a religious procession honoring the Virgen de Rosario. Spectators toss flower petals at the marchers.

November

November 1 and 2 are the Catholic holidays **Día de Todos los Santos** (All Saints' Day) and **Día de los Difuntos** (All Souls' Day), respectively. On these days Catholics honor the saints of the Church and pray for the souls of the faithful departed. Bolivian Indians also use the occasion to carry on the pre-Columbian tradition of honoring their dead ancestors. They ceremonially eat and drink with deceased ancestors, set up memorials to loved ones in their homes, and travel to cemeteries to decorate the graves.

December

Christmas festivities take place nationwide on December 25, with two of the most colorful festivals being held in San Ignacio de Moxos and Sucre. The night before Christmas, families attend midnight Mass services and then eat a traditional Christmas dinner of *picana* (a stew made with beef or veal and cooked in wine and herbs).

Recipes

Picante de Pollo **(Spicy Chicken)**

1 whole chicken (4–5 lbs)
3 lbs peeled potatoes
1 cup green peas
1 large onion, diced
3 tbsp *ají* (Bolivian red chili pepper powder; any red chili powder can be substituted)
1 tbsp paprika
1/2 cup spring onion, chopped
2 tbsp parsley, chopped
1 tbsp coriander, chopped
1/2 cup vegetable oil
Salt and pepper to taste

Directions:
1. Cut the chicken into large portions and place in a pan. Add the salt, spring onion, coriander, and enough water to cover the chicken. Boil for 45 minutes.
2. Boil the potatoes in a separate pan and drain.
3. Lightly boil the peas and drain.
4. In a large pan, lightly fry the onion, ají (or other red chili pepper), paprika, parsley, salt, and pepper until the onion is soft. Add 2 cups of the chicken broth and simmer for 10 minutes. Add the chicken pieces, potatoes, and peas. Simmer for 10 more minutes.
5. Serve with rice and a tomato and onion salad.

Sopa de Maní **(Peanut Soup)**

4 cups beef broth
1 medium onion, chopped
1 tbsp chopped parsley
1 tbsp oil
1/2 cup cooked peas
1 carrot, cooked and chopped (optional)
2 medium potatoes, peeled and cubed
1/2 cup raw peanuts, shelled and ground in blender (you can also use peanut butter, but only as a last resort!)

Directions:
1. In a large saucepan slowly fry the onion, tomato, and parsley until the onion becomes soft.
2. Boil the potatoes.
3. Add the beef broth, peas, carrot, potatoes, and peanuts and simmer without stirring for 30 minutes.
4. Garnish with a small handful of slithers of crispy fried potatoes added to each bowl just before serving.

Salteñas (Bolivian Breakfast Pastries)

Pastry ingredients:
6 cups plain flour
6 tbsp shortening or lard
2 egg yolks
1/2 cup milk
1 tbsp sugar
1 1/2 cups lukewarm water
1 tsp salt

Mix all the ingredients together and knead well. Wrap the dough in a damp cloth and keep refrigerated overnight.

Filling ingredients:
3 tbsp shortening or lard
1 1/2 cups chopped onion
1/2 cup chopped spring onion
1/2 cup ground red *ají* (or any red chili powder)
Salt, sugar, cumin, and oregano to taste
1 lb tender beef, cut into very small pieces
1 1/2 tbsp unflavored gelatin dissolved in 1/2 cup water
1 cup cooked peas
1 cup partially cooked potatoes, cubed
2 tbsp beef marrow or shortening
1/2 cup seedless raisins
2 hard-boiled eggs, cubed
6 black olives, seeded and chopped

Directions:
1. Fry the onion in the shortening and add the *ají*, salt, sugar, cumin, and oregano.
2. Add the meat and cook for a few minutes. Remove from stove and allow to cool.
3. Add gelatin, peas, potato, and marrow or shortening. Mix and refrigerate overnight.
4. The next morning, separate the dough into pieces that will make 3- or 4-inch rounds.
5. Put about 1 heaped tablespoon of the filling on each pastry round and add a few raisins, some egg, and an olive.
6. Brush dough edges with milk or egg to seal. Bring sides up and seal around the top with a rope-like edge. Brush with egg or milk.
7. Put on floured baking trays and bake at 500 degrees for 20–30 minutes. Serve immediately.

Llajua (Bolivian Picante Sauce)

Chili peppers
Tomatoes
Salt

Directions:
1. Cut chili peppers in half and remove seeds.
2. Cut tomatoes in half and squeeze juice and seeds into a separate bowl.
3. Grind the chilies and the tomato pulp on a grinding stone (or chopping board if you don't have a stone) and add salt to taste.
4. Combine the pulp with the tomato juice and seeds in the bowl.
5. Serve with all Bolivian food.

[Source: Adapted from
http://www.bolivia.co.uk/recipes.htm]

Glossary

Altiplano—high plain; a large, flat expanse of land in the Andes extending from Bolivia into southern Peru, northwestern Argentina, and northern Chile.

Alto Perú—Upper Peru, the Spanish name for Bolivia during colonial rule.

campesinos—common people, usually of Native American heritage, who live in the country.

cerro—a Spanish word that means "hill"; but the term is often used in reference to mountains as well.

conquistador—a leader in the Spanish conquest of Central and South America.

cordillera—a mountain range, especially one that is part of a larger system of roughly parallel mountain ranges.

exports—goods that are sold outside the country of origin.

herbicides—chemicals used to kill plants.

imports—goods that are brought into a country from another land for use or sale there.

indigenous—native or original to an area.

llajhua—a hot sauce made from tomatoes and pepper pods.

mestizos—people of mixed Spanish and Native American descent.

Oriente—the lowlands in Bolivia east of the Andes (the Spanish word *oriente* means "east").

privatize—to sell a state-controlled business to private investors.

pre-Columbian—characteristic of, or occurring during, the period of time in the Americas before the arrival of Christopher Columbus.

quinoa—a high–protein grain grown on the Altiplano and used in making bread, stews, and a beverage.

vicuña—a wild relative of the llama and alpaca that lives on the Altiplano.

yuca—a root or tuberous vegetable, also called cassava.

zampoña—a traditional Bolivian flute made of hollow reeds lashed together.

Project and Report Ideas

Make of a topographical map of Bolivia

Illustrate the great contrast in land height between Bolivia's highlands and lowlands by making a map that shows the surface features of the country. Using clay or a flour-and-salt mixture, create and label the following features:

- Andes Mountains, including the Cordillera Occidental and Cordillera Oriental
- Major regions: Altiplano, Yungas, Valles, Oriente
- Major mountain peaks: Sajama, Illimani
- Major rivers, including the Mamoré, Guaporé, Desaguadero, Madre de Dios, Beni, and Pilcomayo
- Major lakes, including Titicaca and Poopó
- Capital cities: La Paz and Sucre

Cross-Curricular Reports

Write one-page, five-paragraph reports answering any of the following questions. Begin with a paragraph of introduction. Then write three paragraphs, each developing one main idea. End with a conclusion that summarizes your topic.

- Why are llamas and alpacas well suited for the Altiplano?
- How did Bolivia lose its access to the sea?
- What are three of Bolivia's chief legal exports?
- What reforms did the Movimiento Nacionalista Revolucionario (MNR) make after the Revolution of 1952?
- Why does Bolivia have a poor transportation network (few paved roads and railroads) and how has this affected the country's economic development?

Project and Report Ideas

Reports

Write one-page reports on any of the following topics:

- South American independence and Simón Bolívar
- The highland center of Tiwanaku
- Cerro Rico and the founding of Potosí
- Camel-like animals of the Andes (llama, alpaca, guanaco, and vicuña)
- South America's deepest lake, Lake Titicaca
- Typical Bolivian dress
- Wildlife of Noel Kempff Mercado National Park
- Andes Mountains
- Inca Indians
- Antonio José de Sucre

Chronology

1400 B.C. –400 B.C.	The first Native American tribes settle in present-day Bolivia.
A.D. 500–900	Tiwanaku Indians establish an empire covering present-day southern Peru, northern Chile, and much of the Bolivian highlands.
1400s	Inca Indians extend their empire into the Bolivian highlands, conquering and assimilating the Aymara tribes.
1531	Spanish conquistadors, led by Francisco Pizarro and Diego de Almagro, arrive in Peru; within two years they will take control of the Inca Empire.
1544	Discovery of silver in Bolivia at Cerro Rico leads to influx of Spanish settlers who take the land and establish mines, forcing Indians to work as slaves.
1809	People of Chuquisaca (later renamed Sucre) launch uprising against Spanish rule on May 25.
1824	Major General Antonio José de Sucre liberates Peru (which includes Alto Perú) in the Battle of Ayacucho, on December 9.
1825	Alto Perú proclaims its independence and is renamed Bolivia, in honor of Símon Bolívar.
1879–84	War of the Pacific; with defeat, Bolivia loses the Atacama Desert and its coastline to Chile.
1932–35	Chaco War with Paraguay results in Bolivia's loss of the Chaco Boreal.
1952	Movimiento Nacionalista Revolucionario (MNR) party installs Víctor Paz Estenssoro as president of civilian government and institutes important reforms.
1964	Military coup ousts MNR party from power.

1967	Bolivian army captures and kills Che Guevara, a revolutionary leader who was trying to instigate a Communist uprising in Bolivia.
1982	Civil rule and democratic government restored to Bolivia with the installation of Hernán Siles Zuazo as president.
1990s	Bolivia's democratic leaders institute reforms to privatize many government-run businesses; with the United States, Bolivia works to disrupt drug trafficking.
2001	Vice President Jorge Quiroga replaces President Hugo Banzer Suárez, who resigns due to ill health.
2002	Bolivia's congress selects Gonzalo Sanchez de Lozada as president by an 84–43 margin over radical Indian leader Evo Morales.
2004	At a summit in Cuzco, Peru, representatives of Argentina, Bolivia, Brazil, Chile, Colombia, Ecuador, Guyana, Paraguay, Peru, Suriname, Uruguay, and Venezuela establish the South American Community of Nations (CSN), a continent-wide political- economic organization modeled on the European Union.
2005	In July, the 12 CSN countries, plus Mexico and Panama, meet in Brazil to analyze citizen-security issues.

Further Reading/Internet Resources

Bolivia (Fiesta! series). Danbury, Conn.: Grolier Educational, 1999.

Herndon, William Lewis. *Exploration of the Valley of the Amazon.* New York: Grove Press, 2000.

Paretzky, Johanna N., and Priya H. Patel, eds. *Let's Go: Peru, Ecuador and Bolivia.* New York: St. Martin's Press, 2001.

Swaney, Deanna. *Bolivia.* Melbourne, Australia: Lonely Planet Publications, 2001.

Travel Information

http://www.boliviaweb.com/cities/index.htm#General
http://www.lonelyplanet.com/destinations/south_america/bolivia/
http://www.ddg.com/LIS/aurelia/boltou.htm

History and Geography

http://lcweb2.loc.gov/frd/cs/botoc.html
http://www.lib.umich.edu/govdocs/foreign.html

Economic and Political Information

http://www.odci.gov/cia/publications/factbook/geos/bl.html
http://www.emulateme.com/bolivia.htm

Culture and Festivals

http://www.andes.org/
http://www.latinworld.com/sur/bolivia/index.html
http://www.boliviaweb.com/recipes/english/

The official promotion and regulating agency for tourism is the Viceministerio de Turismo.

Viceministerio de Turismo
Ministerio de Comercio Exterior e Inversión
Av. Mcal. Santa Cruz
Palacio de las Comunicaciones, Piso 16
Bolivia
Telephone: +591-2-367463 or 367464 or 358213 or 367441
Fax: +591-2-374630
Email: vturismo@mcei.gov.bo

Bolivian Embassy
3014 Massachusetts Ave., NW
Washington, DC 20008
Telephone: (202) 483-4410

U.S. Department of Commerce Trade Information Center International Trade Administration
14th and Constitution Ave., NW
Washington, DC 20230
Telephone: 800-USA-TRADE
Website address: http://www.ita.doc.gov

American Chamber of Commerce in Bolivia
Edificio Hilda, Oficina 3
Avenida 6 de Agosto
Apartado Postal 8268
La Paz, Bolivia
Telephone: (591) 2-43-25-73
Fax: (591) 2-43-24-72
Home Page: http://www.bolivianet.com/amcham

Index

Index/Picture Credits

Contributors

Senior Consulting Editor **James D. Henderson** is professor of international studies at Coastal Carolina University. He is the author of *Conservative Thought in Twentieth Century Latin America: The Ideals of Laureano Gómez* (1988; Spanish edition *Las ideas de Laureano Gómez* published in 1985); *When Colombia Bled: A History of the Violence in Tolima* (1985; Spanish edition *Cuando Colombia se desangró, una historia de la Violencia en metrópoli y provincia*, 1984); and coauthor of *A Reference Guide to Latin American History* (2000) and *Ten Notable Women of Latin America* (1978).

Mr. Henderson earned a bachelor's degree in history from Centenary College of Louisiana, and a master's degree in history from the University of Arizona. He then spent three years in the Peace Corps, serving in Colombia, before earning his doctorate in Latin American history in 1972 at Texas Christian University.

LeeAnne Gelletly is a freelance writer and editor living outside Philadelphia, Pennsylvania. She has worked in publishing for more than 20 years.